Zoo Vet

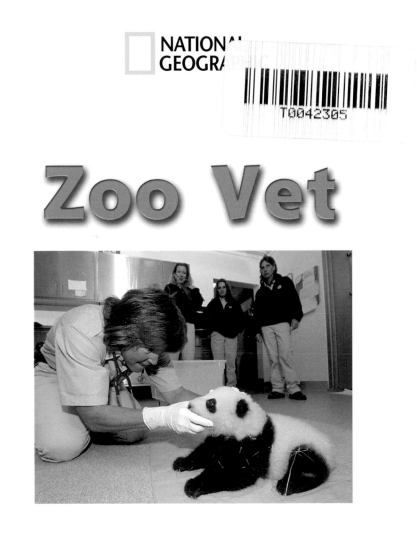

Andrew Einspruch

Contents

The zoo vet checks this lizard ▶
to make sure it is healthy.

Vet Check

Where do you take your pet when it gets sick?
You probably take it to the veterinarian, or vet.
These animal doctors help keep our pets healthy.
Vets also work at zoos. Zoo vets work with all
the different animals at the zoo.

Keeping Animals Healthy

Most of the time, zoo vets help animals stay healthy. This means giving them checkups. They also make sure animals get the right food and get enough exercise.

Checkups

The zoo vet gives each animal at the zoo a checkup every year. The zoo vet weighs the animal during its checkup. The vet checks the animal's eyes, teeth, and feet. The vet also listens to the animal's heart. This helps the vet make sure each animal is healthy.

This baby panda is having ▶ its first checkup.

Vet Tools

Tools the Vet Uses	What the Vet Does
Stethoscope	Listens to animal's heart and breathing
Syringe	Takes a blood sample
Scale	Measures animal's weight
Tooth scaler	Cleans teeth
Clippers	Trims claws

Bong Su is an Asian elephant. He lives in a zoo. Elephants in zoos need to have their feet cleaned and nails trimmed so they don't get cracked and sore.

▼ Bong Su lives in a zoo in Australia.

6

▼ The zoo vet files Bong Su's feet to keep them healthy.

▼ Bong Su keeps his foot still while the vet cleans his nails.

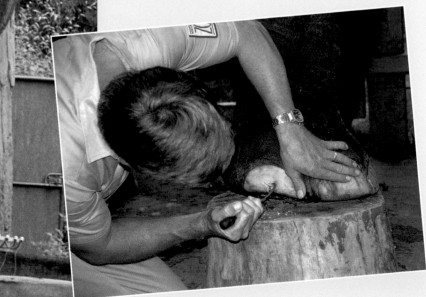

Food

Zoo vets need to know what animals eat in the wild. They make sure each zoo animal gets the right kind of food. The zoo vet also makes sure each animal gets the right amount of food.

Pandas eat ▶
bamboo.

Zoo vets decide what each animal ▶
needs to eat to stay healthy.

Exercise and Play

Animals need exercise, too. They need places to climb or hide. Some animals like to play with toys. Zoo vets and zookeepers try to make sure these animals have things to do during the day.

Zookeepers make ▶
sure bears have
trees and logs
for climbing.

Climbing this slide is good
exercise for a baby gorilla.

Helping Sick Animals

Zoo vets know how sick animals behave. Many sick animals stop eating. Others get grouchy. Animals that are hurt or injured may limp. When an animal gets sick or injured, the zoo vet helps it get better.

This zoo vet is ▶ giving medicine to a sick gorilla.

The zoo vets put this monkey to sleep ▶ so they can check its injury.

Sometimes, an injured animal needs to be asleep so the vet can check it. The vet shoots the animal with a dart. The dart is filled with a drug to make the animal sleepy. The animal's injuries are checked after it falls asleep.

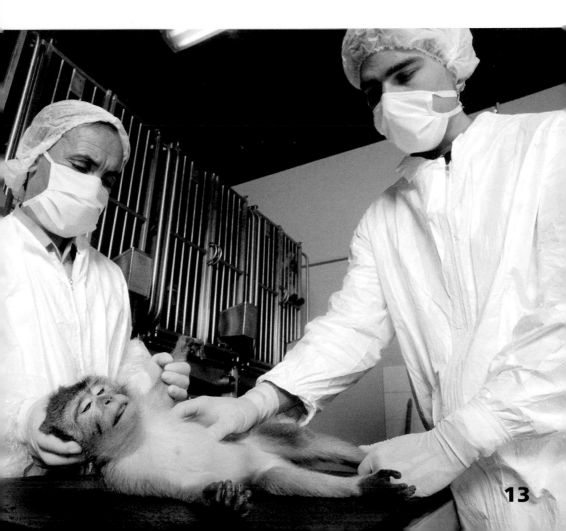

Kashmar is a leopard. She lives in a zoo with her sister. One day Kashmar's eye got cut when the two leopards had a fight. The zoo vet had to check Kashmar's eye.

The vet flushed ▶ Kashmar's eye with water to wash out any dirt.

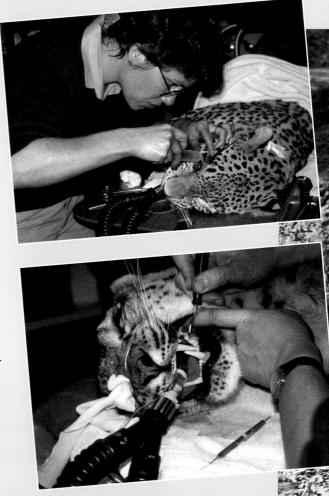

The vet cleaned ▶ Kashmar's teeth during the checkup.

First, the zoo vet put Kashmar to sleep and cleaned her eye. Next, the vet did a complete checkup. Then, the zookeepers moved Kashmar back to her pen. Finally, the vet gave her another drug to wake her up.

▼ Kashmar is back on her feet again.

Zoo for You?

Maybe you'd like to be a zoo vet. Do you love animals? Do you think you'd like taking care of them? If so, being a zoo vet may be the job for you!

▼ If you like animals, you might work in a zoo one day.